BOY GEO
AND CULTURE CLUB

JO DIETRICH

PROTEUS
Rocks

PROTEUS BOOKS is an imprint of
The Proteus Publishing Group

Published and distributed by:
CHERRY LANE BOOKS
COMPANY, INC.,
P.O. Box 430,
Port Chester, NY 10573

United Kingdom
PROTEUS BOOKS LIMITED,
Bremar House, Sale Place,
London W2 1PT

distributed by:
J.M. DENT & SONS
(DISTRIBUTION) LIMITED,
Dunhams Lane, Letchworth,
Herts. SG6 1LF

ISBN 0 86276 235 9 (paperback)

First published in U.K. 1984

Copyright © 1984 Jo Dietrich and
Proteus Books Ltd.

Editor: Kay Rowley

Designed by: Laurence Bradbury
Typeset by: SX Composing,
Rayleigh
Reproduction by: Aragorn Colour
Reproduction
Printed in Great Britain by Blantyre
Printing & Binding, Glasgow

photo credits:
David Corio
Gabor Scott
Virginia Turbett
Steve Rumney
Barry Plummer
Bryn Jones
Syndication International
Laura Levine
Daily Express Syndication
Photofeatures Int.
Aquarius
Howard Tyler
Derek Ridgers/Ace
Chris Walter

CONTENTS

1

'And if the homework brings you down Then we'll throw it on the fire And take the car down town.'

(*Kooks* – David Bowie. Chrysalis Music Ltd/Titanic Music Ltd.)

One fine monday back in 1976, young George O'Dowd walked into school for the last time. It was not the end of term nor was George, accelerated pupil though he was, about to ascend the ivory towers of a university education. The simple facts were these: George had been caught playing truant the previous Friday and responded by turning up late (a habit which was fast approaching a tradition with him) clad in his most comfortable clothes. School uniforms, after all, can be so stuffy. Thus, the fifteen year-old George walked through the portals of Bexleyheath Comprehensive wearing plastic sandals, a pair of baggy trousers purchased from Oxfam and his hair dyed a scintillating shade of orange. The headmaster was not amused.

A worthy soul, George's headmaster was nonetheless deficient when it came to tolerating and indeed, appreciating, the finer points of style in a young man's dress. Rather than hold up young George as an example of all that was good and imaginative in his school, the misguided man offered our hero six of the best. A polite refusal was greeted with headmasterly disdain and a summary notice of expulsion was served on George. George has five brothers, one sister and two parents, one of each sex. Mr. and Mrs. O'Down were Irish, Catholic and very upset with the results of George's act of rebellion. They were quite unprepared for the sequence of events which were eventually to lead our hero to fame and fortune, fronting the most original group to emerge in the eighties – Culture Club.

'When I was about fourteen I was having a really bad time at school,' recalls George. 'I didn't like it at all. I hated all the people and didn't have any friends there. I had a really high voice and people used to laugh at me because they thought I was a bit of a poof. They never hit me though because I had five brothers.

'Anyway, the people I used to go around with were much older, about eighteen, and I started getting interested in things like Bowie, went off to a hairdressing show and came back with my hair bright orange!'

Another reason he was not the most popular boy in school among his male classmates and teachers was the fact that he went around telling everyone he was gay. He attributes this stance and his colourful costume to his basic shyness – a defence mechanism that immediately put him in the limelight as a reaction to being picked on. His teachers were so concerned they eventually sent him to the school psychiatrist to get him 'straightened out'. Funnily enough, the only people he never had any trouble with were girls.

'I used to be *the* person to go out with at school, because I was such a poof. I did think I was David Bowie then. I had big hairy eyebrows . . .'

So what kind of effect was George's errant

Chez, George's dad.

4

SCHOOL'S OUT

lifestyle having at home? Having moved from Ireland to London just before George was born, his parents have since become reconciled to their son's behaviour, especially in the light of his success, but there were days when the domestic harmony of the O'Dowd home was sorely disrupted. George's mother now looks after an old people's home in London and is justifiably proud of her son's achievements but George can recall the days when all was not so pleasant.

'My mother threw plates and toasters at me and told me she hated me, and I did likewise. But a lot of it's not agreeing with what people do, it's understanding why they do it.'

Similarly, George's father, Chez O'Dowd, who used to run a boxing club, took a little time to get used to the fact that one of his five sons intended travelling a route rather less familiar than that of his other four boys.

'I spent a long time in my childhood trying to relate to my father — and I couldn't. Then suddenly, bang, my father grew up at the same time that I did. I can really relate to my parents now. I can have an intelligent conversation, and to me that is valuable.'

'My brothers are boxers, my dad runs a boxing club. My little brother is a South London ABA champion. He's a really good boxer. My dad's really proud of him, but he's also proud of me that I've got a good product, that I've got something. He knows me, he knows what I'm about. He knows that I'm not suddenly going to turn up at the house in a big Cadillac wearing a pink fur coat saying. 'Oh hello. I'm rich.' He knows I'm not going to go off my head, he knows I'm not that sort of person. And I've no wish to be like that, I've no wish to impress anyone.'

With brother Gerald.

2

'George . . . should have a band of his own.'

— Malcolm McLaren.

With the world of institutionalised education behind him, George packed his bags and set off to seek fame and fortune in Birmingham. Here his interest in old clothes led to work on a second-hand clothing stall. It was fun for a while, but George eventually found that communal living was not quite all it was cracked up to be. George is very domestic by nature — 'I love cleaning up' — but the people he lived with did not share his love of tidiness or his deep need for a domestic harmony. Viewing the disarray of the flat in which he was continually picking up after other people, he began to yearn for companions of a more particular nature and the headier nightlife of a less confining city. London crooked a painted fingernail in his direction and George moved south to the City of Sin. Like most people adrift in the metropolis for the first time, George tried his hand at a variety of jobs, changing work as the opportunity offered or the whim took him.

He worked as a painter, a window cleaner, a make-up artist for the Royal Shakespeare Company on the play *Naked Robots,* and as a model in TV advertisements. You might have seen him adorning commercials for the Trustee Savings Bank, Pils Lager or British Airways.

An inveterate club-goer, George hung around the various London clubs, picking up notices in the rock press simply as a result of his colourful presence. He lived in various flats and squats, the most notorious being at Carburton Street, and made friends with the likes of Kirk Brandon, and Matthew Ashman of Bow Wow Wow. Brandon was in the process of disbanding his punk group, The Pack and recruited George for a new project, a band who rejoiced in the name *In Praise Of Lemmings.* In between, George was developing his singing voice by practising with Matthew Ashman and making tapes of songs by singers like Ella Fitzgerald, Shirley Bassey and Pearl Bailey.

The club scene had come a long way since the mid-seventies when the fourteen year-old George could be seen wandering around Chagurama's, the gay club that was later to evolve into the palace of Punk, the Roxy. Billy's, Blitz and the New Romantics held sway by the late seventies and George found himself hanging around with the 'in' crowd — the infamous Marilyn, Jeremy of Haysi Fantayzee, filmmaker John Maybury and Kirk Brandon, who moved into George's squat one accident-prone night at Blitz, where the Boy earned a little make-up money by looking after coats and handbags. Their main concern was the pursuit of pleasure; their most effective weapon in the war against boredom was themselves.

So George would fall out of Blitz at eleven o'clock drunk out of his mind and end up on the cover of *Stern* and *Donna.* Good times!

George even recalls the night David Bowie came down to Blitz to round up people for his *Ashes To Ashes* video.

'He sent this girl down to get people who looked ''weird'' and I was one of them y'know.' And she said, 'DB wants to see you upstairs!' And I said, 'Who's that?' And she whispered in my ear, 'David Bowie'. And I just went, 'Oh yeah . . .'

'I went upstairs and there was this table full of people just grinning blankly surrounded by stupid girls looking dead uncool. I don't know how he can stand it. He must think they're all a load of wankers . . . he must. It must really frighten him, he must have to treat the whole thing like a game of chess.

'A lot of people want to be like David Bowie, they want to be David Bowie. I don't. I think he's had it really. I think he's great, brilliant, but he's just THERE like Harrods or Frank Sinatra. I wasn't asked to do the video. I'm pleased, I wouldn't have done it anyway.'

It was a time of gatecrashing parties at the Embassy or Legends, film premières and getting their pictures in the papers. They preened, pouted and posed, playing at being stars when, of course, they were nothing of the kind. The joke was on us.

Eventually Matthew Ashman asked George if he would like to audition for the singing spot in Bow Wow Wow. They were having trouble with Annabella who kept saying the wrong things in interviews, like how she really wanted to work in a sweet shop or be an air hostess. George went for an audition and they hated him. But the taste of glory was on George's tongue and it was not long before he approached Malcolm

Kirk Brandon

'With Marilyn

MEMBERSHIP

George as a Blitz Kid

McLaren, the Frankenstein of Pop, to try and get into the band.

'Eventually I met Malcolm at Planets, which was this club I was running. I was really drunk and went up to him in stilettos and a big straw hat with birds on and said, 'I really want to sing with Bow Wow Wow and he just *looked*!'

McLaren, who was intent on turning the group into the hottest thing since prawn vindaloo was unhappy with Annabella's persistent refusal to act out his fantasies. In retrospect, George now sees his involvement in Bow Wow Wow as a ploy to get Annabella to buck up her ideas and frighten her into thinking she was going to be replaced. When George walked on stage at the Rainbow fairground concert to sing the encore for Bow Wow Wow in place of Annabella, he got the biggest reception of the evening and prompted even the taciturn Paul Morley to wax lyrical in the *NME*:

'Rumoured to be the new singer, a person called George guested on one rockabilly song amidst a whole pile of old-fashioned encores. George's viperish flamboyance immediately shifted the sexual implications and radically altered visual tension: it was a different group. Annabella is openly unskilled: George is kind of glib. Both possess an amateurism that rubs attractively against the Wow boys' professionalism.'

This and other favourable notices did the trick. McLaren's ruse worked and Annabella pulled her socks up. Naturally, following a successful stage debut, George wanted to know where he stood à propos of Bow Wow Wow. He can now be philosophical about the way McLaren used him, especially as, when asked whether George had joined Bow Wow Wow. McLaren's reply appeared in the music press: 'George isn't part of the band but he should have a band of his own.'

George recalls one of his last encounters with McLaren at the time and explains why he was drafted in the first place. 'Basically they got me in because I wore a lot of make-up and looked a bit effeminate. It was just to frighten Annabella, insult her femininity because she wasn't shaking her tits or lifting her skirt like Malcolm wanted her to. In the end, though, she got better and better and they didn't exactly throw me out, I just went round to see Malcolm and he hid behind the curtains!'

Now he can stand back and analyse the situation without too much acrimony.

'If you're in a situation with Malcolm and you can stand outside that situation and see what he's doing you can get on with him. By being aware of him, you become aware of a lot of other things as well.'

With his first professional singing appearance behind him, and McLaren's words ringing in his ears, Boy George began to muster his forces.

George modelling at a fashion show, St. Martin's School Of Art, 1980.

If George is the voice and face of Culture Club, then drummer Jon Moss is the heartbeat of the group. Jon began playing in bands at school and also became a schoolboy rock concert promoter — early signs of his entrepreneurial ability. Having turned down a place at Cambridge University where he would have studied Greek, Jon tried his hand at a variety of jobs, none of which lasted for more than a few months. He worked for his father who ran a chain of menswear stores called Alkit. He was a printer (like George), a tape operator at the Marquee recording studio and even an apprentice baker. But Jon was first and foremost a drummer and he practiced every evening, playing short-lived stints with jazz-funk bands like Eskimo Norbert and Pastrami Barmy.

Seeing the Sex Pistols gave him a taste for something harder and more upfront and, like George, was given what looked like a 'big break' when he auditioned for a mystery band. Jon tells the story with a laugh.

'Joe Strummer said he couldn't tell me what band it was. So I said, 'You're the Clash.' 'How do you know?' he asked. 'Because it's written on your jacket.'

Impressed by the drummer's perspicacity and ability to read (not a necessary qualification for rock drummers), the Clash hired him. It was not a marriage made in Heaven however, and three months later Jon left. There were arguments over the group's policy which Jon thought of as unrealistic and hypocritical.

'I remember when I played with the Clash,

Roy Hay

I thought Bernard Rhodes was brilliant, he had a lot to say. But I got pissed off with it because they had such strong political attitudes. I told them they couldn't do what they wanted and have their attitudes. I said if you make a million pounds you aren't going to give it to the kids on the street.'

'If I make a million pounds with Culture Club and I want to give some money to Greenpeace or build a hospital wing, I can do it, but I'm not going to say, 'Now I'm doing this so I can make everybody's life better.' I don't believe it and to be in the Clash you had to believe it, so I left. I was all too serious, too desperate. I like freedom in music. Like, when I was with the Damned for six months, I went on to a bottle of beer on the head and a bottle of vodka every night and it's just nowhere. The thing about hedonism is, you just die, you end up in a rut.'

Jon started his own punk group, London, which soon collapsed and he did the punk circuit, drumming for a variety of bands like the Damned, Jona Lewie, the Edge and Adam during his leather-punk *Car Trouble* days. When the seemingly indestructible bubble of punk finally burst, Jon found himself without work, without prospects, and looking into a black hole labelled, 'No Future'.

'After six years of failure, I got depressed and spent six months staring at my bedroom wall.'

Girding up his loins, Jon then tried his hand at the new technology and became a video technician — a skill that was to prove very useful in the future, as he was shortly to be

Mike Craig

3

'Culture Club offers a free membership and it's open to everyone.'

— Boy George

Jon Moss

contacted by George who wanted to discuss the formation of Culture Club. George had been given Jon's name by a mutual friend, Kirk Brandon.

Michael Craig is the only black member of the Club. This is interesting, if only because George originally wanted Culture Club to be an all-black group.

'I originally wanted an all-black band,' he says, 'but to be quite honest, one untogether black person is quite enough and I already knew I wanted Mikey in on bass.'

Known as Mikey to his colleagues and friends, Craig is the oldest member of the band and, according to Roy Hay, the worst at getting up in the mornings. Mikey has two children, Kita (6) and Amber (5) who like having a dad in Culture Club, one of their favourite bands. Sadly, Mikey is now separated from their mother, Cleo, but the family connection is continued to some extent by Captain Crucial (Amos), Cleo's brother, who performs all the Jamaican toasting for the group.

Mikey grew up in the musical environment of the North with a thorough grounding in Northern Soul and was a reggae sessioneer and a sound system owner before meeting George in a club. When Mikey first bumped into George he found him, 'a very interesting character. When you meet someone like that you want to get to know them and find out more about them. I met him in a club about two years ago. I never expected him to be so big.'

And last, but by no means least, there is Roy Hay, the group's guitarist. Roy is by far the quietest member of the group which may also have something to do with the fact that he is the only married man of the four. He recently took the plunge and married his long-standing girlfriend, Alison.

Before he answered George's ad for a guitarist, he had been diligently carving a career for himself in haridressing in Southend and playing guitar and piano in local groups.

When he and Alison tied the knot, the group coughed up for some nice wedding presents.

'Mikey got us a very expensive set of saucepans. Jon and George chipped in together and got us a food mixer. George also got me an outrageous teapot in the style of a rockabilly with a blond quiff. That was the most original one.'

Surprisingly, Roy has nothing to do with George's hairstyle – though he has had a go at the other member's locks.

'I used to cut Jon's and I did the mohican that Mikey used to have. But George created his own. He asked me to do things for it, but I was too scared that I might muck it up.'

Being the quietest member, he was asked recently if he felt any resentment at George getting all the limelight.

A GATHERING OF CULTURES

'Not really. He is the singer and the centre-piece, always will be, and I've known that since we started the band. We all know how important we are to each other behind the scenes.'

George is very articulate about his aims in forming the group and while it is largely his philosophy that has shaped the band, it is also the combination of four people from wildly differing backgrounds who have a common aim that makes Culture Club so succesful.

'I didn't want musos,' says George. 'We haven't got anything in common, it's not the clever little pop package people seem to think it is. I don't say to them, ''Come on, put your Culture Club gear on and let's get up the Palace and be seen,'' because they're not into that — we don't plan things that way.'

'I found Jon through Kirk Brandon from Theatre of Hate. Jon's been in a hell of a lot of bands and I knew I wasn't capable of organis-ing one. I met Michael in a night club. We wanted a guitarist who was just a competent guitar player, never heard of me, ever been to any of the clubs, just someone who was really enthusiastic. I really liked Roy as soon as I met him. He was quiet, didn't have a big mouth.'

'That's how it started. No fairy story.'

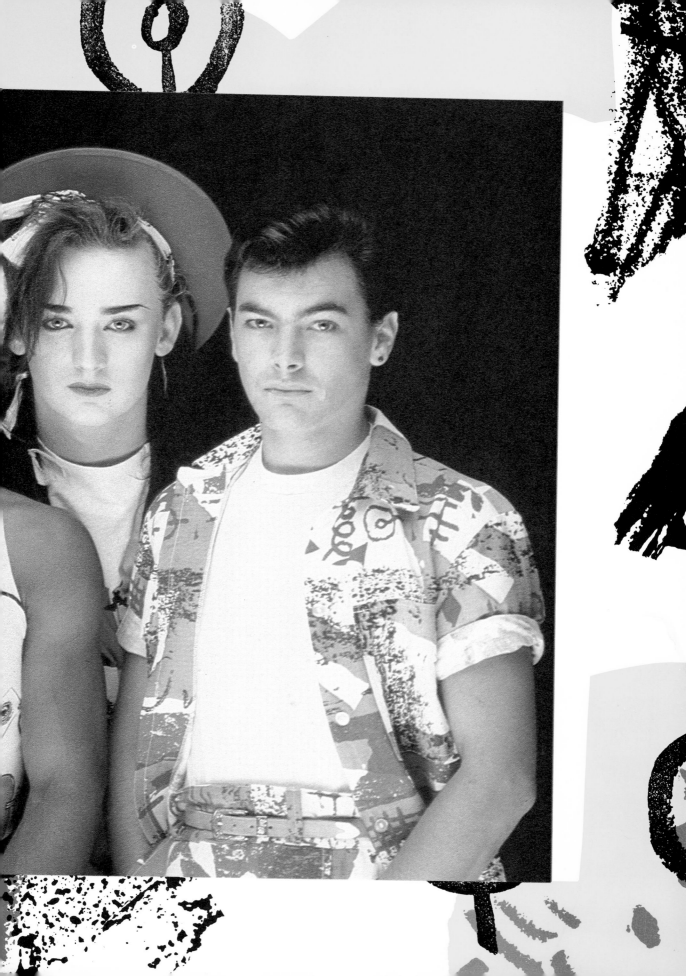

4

'If music be the food of love, play on . . .'

PATHS TO GLORY

'I write the words and I write the melodies. I get an idea and I just sort of sing it and I keep singing it until Roy gets the idea and Jon arranges things and Mikey puts his bass line down. Mikey's starting to get some good ideas now, we're all more into the musical side of things. I've never known anything about music. For someone like me to write a song and get to number three just shows that anybody can do it. Anyone can do something, it's just whether you get up and do it. I used to spend a lot of time just pissing about and now I've actually concentrated on doing something. Whether it would be successful or not is beside the point with me.'

When Culture Club was formed, in April 1981, Bucks Fizz was at number one with *Makin' Your Mind Up.* The post-punk boom was well and truly dead and buried in a lead-lined coffin and music had separated into a multitude of new structures with well-crafted pop songs once again taking the lead in the charts. The time was right for imaginative groups to draw on a variety of sources and musical forms to shape their own identity. People were looking back before going forward. Groups like Kid Creole and the Coconuts were looting musical history and fusing it with an individual style to produce bright musical collages that blew away all

notions of 'purity' and 'roots' and other once fashionable precepts that had held back the progress of pop music for so long. It became harder and harder to label groups — the 'reggae' group, the 'soul' group, the 'African' group, the 'rock and roll' group — titles became meaningless. Among others, Dexys Midnight Runners scored a notable success with their incredible blend of Stax Soul and Celtic rhythms.

So when Culture Club began the arduous task of selecting their material in studios and rehearsal rooms in the Goldhawk Road, the group had no preconceptions about what style of music they would be playing. Mind you, their early gigs weren't always marked by success. Audiences unaccustomed to the sound and the look of the band would often interrupt their set with yells of 'Queers!' and other ill-informed critical remarks.

'When we first started playing gigs,' recalls George, 'we were terrible, so bad we were brilliant — we did a gig in Chadwell Heath and got heckled by this builder who called me a fucking queer. I walked off without finishing the gig and the band were screaming at me.'

Nevertheless, having taken the plunge, they then got themselves a manager, Tony Gordon — a real businessman who, claims George, fitted their image of a business manager.

They built up a sizeable following in the south-east, playing a number of sell-out gigs in Southampton, Brighton and London, notably at Heaven where they went down, as the saying goes, a storm.

Record company offers began to flood in and they settled for Virgin Records, not because it was the most money (it wasn't), but because the group liked the attitude of the staff and the company policy as a whole.

If George is the figurehead of Culture Club, then Jon is definitely the power behind the throne. George freely admits Jon's massive contribution to the group.

'When Jon came along it was a real shambles, my songs were like artschool poems — though I've never been to art school believe me — but they were sort of twenty paragraphs, pages and pages of words. I'm really lyrical but Jon said, 'where's the chorus, where's the beginning, where's the ending?' And that was something we learned together.'

'Also we went to a lot of record companies and got ourselves studio time, which was easy to get because of the way I looked. A lot of people had seen me with Bow Wow Wow at the Rainbow but weren't sure what to make of us, so Jon's attitude was to get them to pay for as many demos as possible.'

In his turn, Jon is candid about his relationship with George within the group and remembers when he first met him.

'I thought he was really naff, but I thought

he was pretty. I still think the same as I thought then, that he wouldn't stop talking, and it was impossible to get any sense out of him, and he used to say about thirty things in one sentence, and his patience is about that big (putting finger and thumb a fraction apart). I thought, 'This is going to be a really hard job. But, on the other hand, I also thought he was a genius. I think he's a creative genius with words and images.'

'The only thing George lacks is the ability to take full control of himself, but I think if he did take full control of himself, he wouldn't be like he is.'

'I saw in George something that was lacking in me, but something that I could add to. I'm quite a conservative person. I can take his chaos and put it into order, but without his chaos I can sink to a very low level.'

Gradually in rehearsal and during several

fraught gigs, the songs began to take shape. Because there was so much music available, influences were never finite. George had been listening to Bowie and Bolan at school and had made a few tapes with Matthew Ashman of songs by the likes of Ella Fitzgerald and Shirley Bassey. And the Boy's tastes are still incredibly varied – Cliff Richard, Julio Iglesias, Haysi Fantayzee, Fleetwood Mac – it comes down to the quality of the individual song. Small wonder is it that Culture Club's music should defy classification.

'I'd never written a song before,' says George of those early days, 'just had loads of ideas in my head. Like just when you're walking down the road, your footsteps are a natural beat and anyone with any imagination at all can fill in the gaps and write a song, it's the easiest thing in the world. But the early songs evolved mainly from Roy's guitar from my basic idea because I had no clear idea of what I wanted them to sound like. So the band just used to riff about until they'd built up the idea into a full song – that's how *White Boy* came about.'

White Boy was Culture Club's debut single – an antidote to the inverse racialism that saw hip young men mouthing off about how they were into Bob Marley and how some of their best friends were black.

'Hey Devil kiss me/I'm taking chances/Not faking my culture/The rhythm it dances/I love your wisdom/I love your mind/White Boys are babies (not my kind).'

It did absolutely nothing in the charts and they followed it up quickly with *I'm Afraid Of Me*, which suffered a similar fate. It was when they released *Do You Really Want To Hurt Me?* that Culture Club stopped wandering around in the lower depths of the charts

and blazed a trail to number one.

A soulful ballad, *Do You Really Want To Hurt Me?* crossed barriers, struck chords in many hearts and was bought by teenagers and grannies alike. It is, categorically, one of the great pop singles of the eighties.

'*Do You Really Want To Hurt Me?* is a song, written as a song,' explains George. 'It's probably the only proper song we've got, with proper chord sequences and keyboard changes in it. It's just very musical. I think it's a very well constructed song.'

Not only is it a good song but it is exceptionally well sung – something of a surprise when one understands that George suffers from asthma and occasionally has problems with his breathing. This accounts for the husky, rather breathy delivery that characterises his style. Although he has learnt to train his voice to fit the lyrics, George does experience some difficulty in the studio.

'I can only sing a song once in the studio, after that it goes. The vocals on *I'm Afraid Of Me* and *White Boy* were demos, because when it came to doing them again I couldn't do it. The funny thing is that I really like playing live and I can do it then. It's partly to do with the buzz you get from an audience. It's important because the only way you can find out people's response to what you are doing is to get out and play.'

And that is precisely what they did. By the summer of '82, they were picking up rave notices in the rock press for their live performances, including several in the prestigious pages of the NME.

'Culture Club are stand-up drums and white dungareed guitar, a hard-handed bass that never gets heavy-handed and . . . Boy! That George can sing. 'Just take a look at me/I couldn't look much better.' George is a wonderful thing alright.'

'There's steel in that sound, stealing its way past the lexicon of love with an unmistakeable look of joy. It's a loving construction illustrating the Culture Club's ability to spin the spotlight from guitar to bass to drums to horns with almost criminal ease. Funk it up, salsa it down and dub that thing out of sight. This is the tonic for 1982's club country.'

'Boy George. What can I say? Deb or dandy, I still only expect a Sylvain or at the most a surrogate Ferry (is there any difference?) but not for one minute did I expect to be confronted with a hot Tamla-beat soul goddess. Or should that be a god?'

Yet another reviewer was caught unawares by the sheer quality of The Club in performance.

'George sings – that was always the big surprise after the fashionable hype. He's the direct antithesis of Yazoo's geniune soul, wrapping mere acceptance in new colours and insignia and proving the way you look is

still important.'

And, a month later, David Dorrell was caught up in the entrancement of the group and its frontman.

'That coy, boy smile has won this crowd. No wonder then that over his shoulders he sports his brother's boxing gloves.'

Those smirks, those solid gloves, the truth is as obvious as the symbolism; 'Man' George has come home to proclaim and protect his title: Mr. Boss Man, The Champ.'

The next two singles, *Time (Clock Of The Heart)* and *Church Of The Poisoned Mind,* on which George shares vocals with the powerfully-voiced Helen Terry, saw Culture Club establishing themselves as the premier pop group of the eighties, confident enough to tackle the incomparable sound of Tamla Motown, wise enough not to ape it.

Already George is being dubbed 'a soul singer' by the denizens of the music press and while it is a well-deserved accolade, it is still an attempt to define what is, in effect, indefinable. Culture Club make love songs – Love is the single most source of inspiration for George – but to avoid further attempts to label him and box him away in a neat musical pigeonhole, he is busy writing songs with other performers in mind. The next album contains titles like *Look No Strings,* written with Musical Youth in mind (firm favourites of George who wanted to share a *Smash Hits* cover with the group but were prevented from doing so by their record company); *Black Money* has been written for Joe Cocker and *Beat Boy Surrender* for Diana Ross. And even if all the songs end up on the Culture Club album there will be no denying the variety of the group's inspiration and output.

Time will tell.

5

'Fa Fa Fa Fa Fashion...'

From Bolan to Bowie, from Adam to Toyah, pop idols have always inspired the imitation game. That is, it's not enough to buy the records, go to the concerts and swap pin-ups, if you're a fan the sincerest form of flattery is to dress like your idol as well.

Whenever Culture Club played it was a safe bet that the audience would be a mass of wide-brimmed, low-crowned black hats — worn on the very back of the head — essential headgear for members of the Club.

Jon Moss bought George's hat for him in Golders Green. Jon is Jewish and the hat is a proper Orthodox Jewish one which high-lighted the religious aspect of the Culture Club look. Further evidence of the thought that went into the group's clothes are the designs by Sue Clowes that the Club wore both on and off stage. When George first came on the scene with Culture Club, he could be seen sporting white vestments emblazoned with venerable Judaeo-Christian symbols dominated by the Star of David which is a common symbol for both Jews and Rastafarians. The Star of David was Jon's idea and co-designer Sue Clowes found the Hewbrew maxim which states: 'Culture And Education, Movement Of All People'. She also added the wreath of roses which surrounds it to symbolise England. Although they've long since abandoned the Star of David because of its possible inter-pretation as a political statement, the clothes were still a kind of multi-ethnic wardrobe that

Jon and George wanted in the first place — symbolising or representing all the ethnic minorities of the world. Culture Club is, after all, open to everyone.

As for the fans who dress exactly like George — dubbed 'Culture Club Clones' by a cynical press — they are predominantly female, and as many black CCCs as white. George is touched by their imitation.

'It's great! Anyway, I think when people call people clones that's bullshit, because everybody picks up on other people's ideas, and I think there's a sort of feeling in the air at the moment.'

'You get kids coming to the gigs; they've got loads of make-up on, they've got their hair in wool, they are trying to look like us, but I think when you get people doing it because they're into it and they're enjoying them-selves that's great. When you get people popping into the shop with their hair in dread-locks, exactly the same hat as me, and they sneer at me and act like they're a big bit of shit about town, I just think that's really de-pressing. I don't go around saying I started it and I did it first, and I don't expect other people to do that either.'

While George is interested in clothes, he is not really caught up in the fashionable merry-go-round. Clothes for him and the rest of the group are a way of expressing themselves individually and collectively. There was no intention to create a fashion movement like, for example, Steve Strange, with whom

January 1981 at the opening of The Wall club in Oxford Street. Facing George is Andy Polaris from Animal Nightlife

George has often been erroneously compared. George once said something to the effect that if any of the group turned up in an Anthony Price suit they would be asked to join another band.

George met Sue in a shop in Covent Garden called Street Theatre where she sold her designs and he worked as a window dresser. Sue's individualist ideas, which had formerly included such striking creations as the Molotov Cocktail — a cocktail dress with the back blown off — and the Gravediggers Suit which featured one muddy leg, one entwined with roses and a veiled hat, were being developed and sold on her stall in Kensington Market. Her work was encouraged by an enthusiastic George who particularly liked her hand-painted ties.

Street Theatre's owner was encouraged to give her designs a more established outlet and The Foundry was born. Her later designs were very much in keeping with the Culture Club minority look — the use of tramps' secret signs on long flowing robes. How this has gone down beneath the arches of Charing Cross has yet to be discovered; it depends, I suppose, on what the secret signs actually means. But it is another aspect of the fusion of new and old cultures which has been tapped by the ever inventive Clowes.

George's attitude to the Club style has been well documented. 'It's basically workman's fabrics with provocative patterns. A very clean, very spiritual, very unsexy-look. It comprises of symbols that represents all the peoples that are looked down on, Rastas, Pakistanis, Jews, Tramps or Hobos.'

'The whole point was to come up with something that was summery and colourful as well as being hard. And we got a really good response from the Star of David shirts so we just took it from there. But we were not trying to say anything, it's just a clever idea. That tribal thing was all a bit obvious really, but when Sue came up with the tramps' symbols it was great. Because you don't imagine tramps having their own secret language. I'd never seen anything like that until Sue showed me it, I'd never even have guessed it existed. It's not necessarily to do with the band, because a lot of people who buy it don't like the band. And the band don't dress up in it all the time. The band wear whatever they want.'

George is no longer an active partner in the shop, though he maintains a close association.

'That's Sue's bag now — I just want to concentrate on Culture Club, getting that to grow.'

Perhaps the most interesting aspect of the Culture Club look is that anyone can wear it. You don't have to be as thin as Twiggy to look good, and many of the designs can be knocked up at home on mum's sewing machine by anyone with a bit of imagination.

Sue Clowes puts her finger on the wide appeal of the clothes when she talks about her most successful model.

'Everything has to be extra large for George. He won't have short sleeves because he's got short fat hairy arms, and dresses have to be made to suit his figure — so they don't make his bum look big or whatever. And the prints have to be much brighter for him.'

Truly, the Club is for everyone — the long and the short and the tall, the fat and the thin. All you need is a little imagination and a lot of nerve.

At Imagination's Coconut Grove party with Scott from Minipops.

Sing if you're glad to be George

Boy George is the first genuinely androgynous pop star. He appears to be neither boy nor girl but some indeterminate, invented sex between. The 'Boy' of his name came about when there was evidently some confusion about his gender and he just got tired of being referred to as 'her'. Yet the predominantly female following of Culture Club regards George as a friend much more than a sex symbol. Sure, they hang about outside his flat whenever they can get hold of his address, they go crazy at concerts and they imitate his dress and make-up but their behaviour, it seems, stems from genuine affection more than from any predatory sexual instinct.

Some quotes from his fans illustrate the point:

'I'd like him to tickle me with his dreadlocks.'

'I'd like George because he's so sweet and gentle.'

'I just want to cuddle him.'

George's songs are, after all, about love and pain and happiness, not sex and drugs and rock and roll.

When he was at school, George used to go around telling everyone he was gay. When asked now whether he is, he states simply that he is bisexual – he likes both men and women. But George does not regard himself as sexy or a sex object. He wants to be liked and, like most normal, rational human beings, would like to maintain a warm loving relationship with any one person at any one time.

And Culture Club's songs reflect that attitude.

'I deal in love,' says George. 'And when I think about love it goes beyond the playground. Some people never grow up in that sense, they think love is just sleeping with someone. When I was at school I didn't giggle when blokes said, 'I screwed her' – I thought it was horrible. I won't have people doing that around me. It's just respect for people.' 'I fall in love all the time. Twenty-four hours a day. I fall in love with people for really silly reasons. I think people should fall in love

With Capital Radio's Gary Crowley

(l to r) Steve Strange, August Darnell and George in 1982

With Coati Mundi (from Kid Creole)

George and his journalist friend Miko leave Heathrow en route for the San Remo Music Festival, February 1984.

a lot. It's great, wonderful. I think it's good and healthy to be in love with people. I always go out with very nice people and I really love all of them. Not mentioning any names . . .'

And George, to his credit, has never mentioned any names. He is not a 'kiss and tell' artist. 'I would never ever sell my sex life to the papers. Everyone I've ever loved I'll love till I die!'

'I'm not a sexual person. I don't think I'm sexy.'

Even when asked direct questions by journalists about his sex life, George retains his good humour and discretion by avoiding names or answering questions like 'Are you gay?' with typical candour.

'Well, to a local bricklayer I suppose I would be . . . I don't really know because I've never not done one or the other. When I was at school I used to go with girls all the time, it was like an obsession. I used to be the person to go out with at school, because I was such a poof.'

'Everybody enjoys sex. It's a human thing, it's like eating and pissing and sleeping, everybody enjoys it. Certain people find it upon themselves to be hip and say that they don't but I don't think anybody just doesn't enjoy sex.'

'All the other countries are really frightened about the LP cover because a lot of people just think I'm a girl. Of course, I enjoy that, I love it! It's great because I've got a certain female element in my character. But I'm not a poof. I'm effeminate in the way I look but I'm not an effeminate person. I don't

like effeminate people.'

'I'm not a transvestite. Everyone thinks I am, but I'm not. I wear Y-fronts. I'm a man! I'm quite manly, actually. I don't think I'm as poofy as I'm made out to be. I'm not gay or anything like that.'

Nevertheless, George did consent to an interview with *Gay News,* who showed more than a passing interest in the rising young pop star. Despite much opposition from the rest of the band, George maintained his articulate code of honour and candour and the interview did no harm at all to the group.

'Look, I fancy women and I fancy men. I'm free to do whatever sexual things I want to do. The whole reason I don't go to gay clubs regularly is because I don't fit in. I don't feel like I want to be part of that. Like, my idea of being a free person is to do and be what you want. And the fact that I might do it in Tesco's or in Bang – be me – is beside the point.'

So despite his appearance, or maybe because of it, George is very much a man. He may sleep with both sexes but he is by no means a gay liberationist in the same way as, for example, Tom Robinson. George is a people liberationist.

He doesn't set himself up as a preacher. There is no dogma in Culture Club.

'It's a bad thing for me to say to kids, 'You should be gay.' It's a big decision for a young kid. I was an ahead child. But a lot of kids aren't and they shouldn't be rushed. I don't even think the age of consent should be lowered. If it were to be, I think a lot of kids could easily be exploited.'

IMPRESSIONS AND IMAGES: FACTS AND *Fancies*

Boy George sporting short hair and make-up doing the clubs by night and posing for photographs outside the infamous Carburton Street squat by day with Marilyn, Jeremy from Haysi Fantayzee and other artists, friends and lovers . . .

Coronation Street is George's favourite television programme. Perhaps he identifies with Bet Lynch . . .

Boy George earning his keep at Blitz looking after coats and handbags . . .

The boy George lookalike in the video for *Church Of The Poisoned Mind* is Siobhan, his sister . . .

Boy George and Marilyn wandering into Hazel O'Connor's *Breaking Glass* reception like stars and spending the entire evening in the Gents afraid to come out except for the odd photograph or two . . .

Boy George staring into the mirror saying, *Do You Really Want To Hurt Me?* . . .

Letters and poems from grandmothers including one from a 'really old woman who wants a T-shirt because she can't afford one on her widow's pension' . . .

Boy George models his vocal style on Stevie Wonder . . .

Do You Really Want To Hurt Me? was not written about Kirk Brandon . . .

George has around five hundred dolls — all gifts from fans — from which he cannot bear to be parted . . .

Do You Really Want To Hurt Me? has been recorded by Rita Coolidge and Ippu-Do . . .

Inspired by Jordan's performance in Jubilee, George dressed up as Boadicea complete with Union Jack shield, a fork, stilettos and a huge hat and stands outside Buckingham Palace as the crowd waved and cheered him in 1980 . . .

George is not a practising Catholic but he does believe in GOD . . .

7

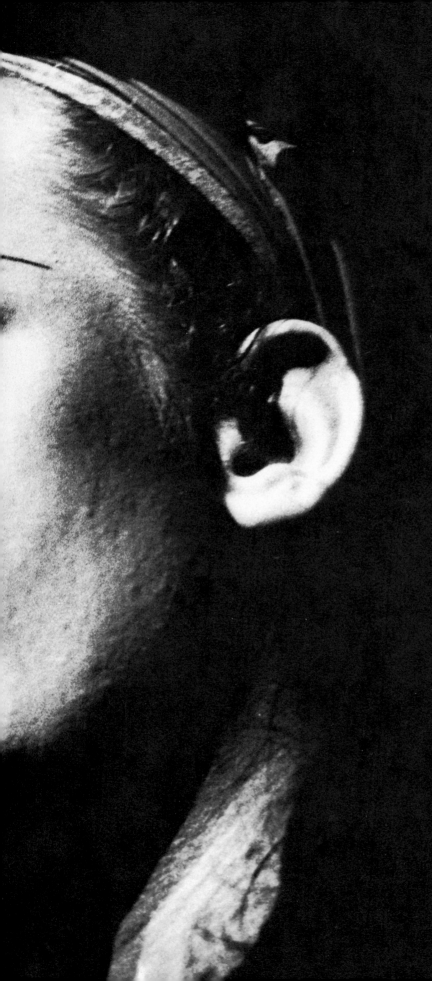

8

Addenda
CULTURE CLUB, ADDENDA

The question is, how long will Culture Club manage to survive? The pop world is littered with the wreckage of one, two and sometimes three hit wonders who, for one brief moment, had the World at their feet and are now back on the treadmill of recording music that doesn't sell and playing gigs that don't sell out. The pop market is among the most unpredictable and the pop audience among the most fickle in the history of recorded sound.

Having been heralded as 'The group of the decade,' Culture Club are going to have to pull out all the stops to maintain the level of success they have attained to date. Yet even as 1983 drew to a close, they managed to produce their most successful single to date in the infectious *Karma Chameleon* – a kind of exuberant affirmation of Boy George's own lifestyle – and the rather more downbeat *Victims,* which were both taken from their second album, *Colour By Numbers.*

The strengths of the group have so far outnumbered their weaknesses. The songs continue to be original and catchy and George is always looking for new avenues to explore writing. Similarly, the importance of a highly developed visual style, especially in terms of pop videos, has allowed Culture Club an almost infinite range of expression and invention. The real problem, as one Adam Ant found to his cost, is how to keep reinventing a style which isn't going to go out of fashion five minutes after it has appeared. To this end, Boy George is already making subtle changes in his attire and look. In place of the familiar round bonnet we can now see a grossly exaggerated top hat adorning our hero's bonce, while the other members of the group have been depicted wearing white morning suits. Shades of the Beatles circa Abbey Road! Doubtless, Jeremy of Haysi Fantaysee will have something to say about George's return to the exaggerated Dickensian garb which he popularised along with his partner, Kate Garner.

But George is a bright boy and he knows

the pitfalls and pratfalls of pop stardom that await him. Having been voted The World's Most Eligible Bachelor by the Society of Women Bachelors in 1983, he is not likely to do anything that might threaten his status as The Boy You Love To Love for some time yet. And George is spreading his wings into record production and helping out on other people's material, notably Helen Terry, with whom he sings on her solo LP to be released later this year.

Whatever the critics may say, and some of them have been a mite unkind about *Victims* — referring to it in the same breath as The Boomtown Rat's overblown *I Don't Like Mondays* — Culture Club are at the height of their powers and their creativity and popularity shows no signs of drying up. Time will tell which of the two will decline first. The only man who has weathered that argument so far is David Bowie.

Perhaps the most significant comments have come from others in the business who have looked at the Culture Club phenomenon and passed judgement:

'The singer I'm most impressed with is Boy George. He's got the most soulful voice that I've heard in years.' Rod Stewart.

'Do You Really Want To Hurt Me? is the kind of record that could have been a hit years ago. His is a curious mixture of unusual looks and very straightforward records, which is clever. I like what he does and if he wrote me a song I would certainly record it.' — Petula Clark.

'He has a superb voice in the old-fashioned sense of having a good voice. I can see him developing into a chameleon character like David Bowie did in the seventies. He has a lasting quality in his voice, and the other lasting quality is that he is interesting, witty and makes sense,' — Mike Read.

'Boy George is one of the more memorable people of the new breed of talent. He has a much better voice than half the others around, and definitely has a future, especially with the large following he has built up from his stage appearances.' — George Martin (ex-Beatles record producer).

Boy George and Culture Club: Built to Last. It is a nice thought.

Culture Club Birthdays:

George — 14 June 1961

Roy — 12 August 1961

Jon — 11 September 1957

Mikey — 15 February 1960

Culture Club Fan Club.

Culture Club,
Wedge Music,
63 Grosvenor St.,
LONDON W1.

At Heathrow leaving for a tour of Canada and the US, March 1984